In the time of Michelangelo

THE RENAISSANCE PERIOD

© Aladdin Books Ltd 2001

Designed and produced by
Aladdin Books Ltd
28 Percy Street
London W1P 0LD

*First published in
the United States in 2001 by*
Copper Beech Books,
an imprint of
The Millbrook Press
2 Old New Milford Road
Brookfield, Connecticut 06804

ISBN 0-7613-2455-0 (lib. bdg.)
ISBN 0-7613-2284-1 (pbk.)

*Cataloging-in-Publication
data is on file at the
Library of Congress*

Editor
Liz White

Design
Flick, Book Design and Graphics

Picture Research
Brian Hunter Smart

Printed in the U.A.E.

In the time of
Michelangelo

Antony Mason

Copper Beech Books • Brookfield, Connecticut

Contents

Introduction

Michelangelo lived in Italy during an exciting period of progress and change in Europe. We now call this period the Renaissance, from a French word meaning rebirth. Michelangelo was not only a painter, he was also a sculptor, architect, and poet. He is considered to be one of the greatest masters of the Renaissance.

Starting in the 1300s, the Renaissance was a time when scholars, sculptors, and painters rediscovered the great works of ancient Greece and Rome—their philosophy, literature, science, architecture, and art. This inspired them to ask questions about the world around them. They began to investigate how the world really works and looks.

Artists and sculptors rapidly developed new skills in sculpture and more realistic and ambitious ways to paint. As the artists became more skilled, they gained in confidence and technical ability and produced some of the finest works the world has ever seen.

Medieval Manuscript Illumination

The medieval period lasted roughly from 500 AD until the mid-1400s. Throughout this period, almost all the painters and sculptors in Europe worked for the Church. The Church was wealthy and powerful. Monks and priests were in charge of all education and schools, as well as book production and libraries. Books were made by hand, painstakingly copied out and often beautifully illustrated—or "illuminated"—with paintings.

Miniature Masterpieces

Working quietly in their monasteries, the artist-monks developed many important skills for drawing and painting. They knew how to draw faces, people, plants, animals, and objects. They could put these together in convincing and attractive compositions. They also had some understanding of perspective—the way that objects appear smaller the farther away they are.

Some of the most beautiful early manuscript illuminations were made for the court of the Frankish emperor Charlemagne (c.742–814), who ruled over much of Europe from his base at Aachen, now in western Germany. Monks continued to improve their artistic skills for the next six centuries, producing extraordinary work. Many of the foundations for the development of European art were laid in these books.

Above: An illuminated manuscript, made in Italy in the 1300s.
Right: Dice-makers, illustrated in a 13th-century book of songs by the Spanish king Alfonso X ("the Wise").

6

Books were carried around and copied by other monks. This meant that the techniques of drawing and painting used to make the manuscripts could also be shared.

The monks stopped producing illuminated manuscripts only after the invention of printing in the 1400s. Suddenly it became much easier and cheaper to produce books on a printing press, so the slow and painstaking work of the manuscript illuminator was no longer needed.

The "paper" used for illuminated manuscripts was made of thin sheets of animal skin or parchment. The writers, called scribes, wrote the words first, using inks and dip-pens, leaving spaces for the paintings.

The artists applied paint with fine brushes made of animal hair. Their paints were made from plant material or minerals, such as iris sap (green), lead (red), soot (black), and the semiprecious stone lapis lazuli (light blue). Gold was also applied in very fine sheets and attached to the page with gum.

Painting for the Church

Christians liked to decorate the interior of their churches; carvings, mosaics, paintings, and stained glass all brightened up the church, and made the space seem richer, more magical. Monks, especially in northern Europe, had shown their ability to create beautiful paintings on a tiny scale in their illuminated manuscripts. But large-scale paintings remained stylized. Many were delicate and were destroyed by damp and age. A change came in Italy in the 1200s, when artists brought fresh inspiration to their larger pieces, and used more lasting techniques such as fresco and tempera. With fresco, they painted in wet plaster directly onto the walls. With tempera, a water-based paint mixed with egg yolk, they painted on wooden panels.

Wall Paintings

One of the first early masters of fresco painting was an artist from Florence, in Italy, called Giotto di Bondone, known simply as Giotto (c.1267–1337). He did two famous series of paintings. The first is in the Arena Chapel, which was built by a rich merchant named Enrico Scrovegni, in Padua, near Venice. It illustrates the life of the Virgin Mary and her family, and the death of Christ. The second series portrays the life of the ever popular St. Francis (c.1180–1226) at the Basilica of St. Francis in Assisi, in Italy.

A group of angels, from Giotto's Adoration of St. Francis (c.1300), one of the series of frescoes in the Basilica of St. Francis, Assisi.

8

Both series create a richly decorative effect. It is as though the walls of the church are covered with colorful wallpaper—but without any repeated patterns. The pictures also tell a story, like a comic strip. But what set Giotto apart from other artists was the new sense of drama and emotion that he put into his paintings.

Earlier artists had been content to paint flatter, more stylized images. Giotto's figures, on the other hand, look three-dimensional and rounded, with individualized faces and carefully painted, realistic-looking clothes. They look like real people. Giotto had a major influence on later painters in Florence, and many of the traditions of European painting can be traced back to his work.

Above: The Dream of Joachim (the father of the Virgin Mary) (c.1303–1305), a fresco by Giotto in the Arena Chapel, Padua.

Below: Maestà (Madonna of the Angels), an altarpiece by Cimabue, painted on wood in about 1275.

Altarpieces

The altar is the main focus of a Christian church and the center of devotion and worship. Special paintings were made to decorate the altar area, and to act as a focus for prayer. Usually these were not painted on the walls themselves, but on planks of wood, using tempera.

Altarpieces featured key figures in the Christian faith, such as Jesus Christ, the Virgin Mary (the Madonna), the Apostles, and the saints and martyrs. Many of the skills of manuscript illumination were used to create these altarpieces, including the application of gold leaf for the background and the saints' halos.

The front panel from Duccio's Maestà (Madonna Enthroned) (1308–1311), in Siena.

Cimabue and Duccio

One of the greatest early painters of altarpieces was Cenni de Pepo, known as Cimabue (c.1240–1302), who also painted frescoes. Details of his life are vague, and it is not certain which paintings are really his. He worked in Florence, and is thought to have painted several important religious works, including several Maestà. Literally meaning "Majesty," Maestà is the term used to describe a painting of the Madonna on a throne holding the child Jesus, surrounded by saints and angels. Like Giotto, Cimabue is credited with bringing a more natural look to human figures.

When Duccio's Maestà was completed, it was paraded from the artist's studio to the cathedral to celebrate Siena's victory over Florence in battle.

One of the most famous altarpieces of the time was painted for the cathedral of nearby Siena by Duccio di Buoninsegna, known simply as Duccio (worked c.1278–1319). It is painted on two sides: on one side is a large Maestà, and on the other the main section shows 26 scenes depicting the Passion—the series of events leading to, including, and following Christ's crucifixion. Duccio's work, like Giotto's, brought a new sense of realism to his paintings. They inspired artists to seek ways to paint images that imitated the real world.

Fresco and tempera

Fresco means "fresh" in Italian: it was a way of painting on a wall using fresh, wet plaster. First, the artists made a sketch on the wall using charcoal, and then the lines were painted over with a red color called sinopia.

Next, the design was covered in a layer of fine wet plaster. The colors were applied using paints made of powdered color mixed with water. In this way, the color was absorbed into the wall, then dried with the plaster, leaving a hard, permanent surface.

With tempera, artists used similar paints, mixed with water and "tempered" with some kind of gum or glue, usually egg yolk. It was used for panel painting, before oil painting began to replace it in the 1400s. Colors were limited, and had to be built up layer upon layer.

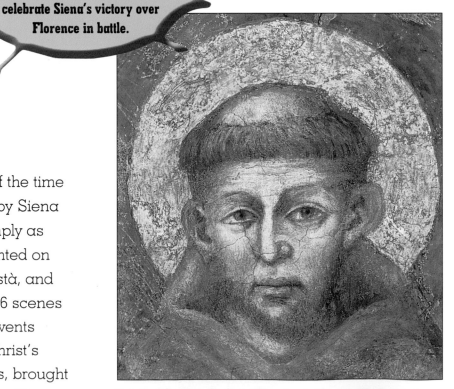

Detail of St. Francis, from Cimabue's Maestà (Enthroned Madonna with St. Francis), a fresco in the Church of St. Francis, Assisi. It shows how fresco artists created shadow by using fairly rough brushstrokes of deeper color.

Around the World
Islam

While Christians were decorating their churches in richly colored scenes from the Bible, Muslim artists were taking a different course. Fearing the worship of false gods, the early leaders of the Islamic religion discouraged artists from illustrating people or animals. Instead, Muslim artists devised patterns of extraordinary complexity and beauty. They used these designs to decorate their mosques, books, and carpets.

Islamic Style

Islam was founded by the Prophet Muhammad (c.570–632), and it spread rapidly by conquest into Asia and across North Africa, reaching Spain in 711 AD. At first, the artists and architects of this new religion adopted the styles of the conquered lands. But by about 850 AD they had developed a

Painted marble decoration at the I'timad al-Dauba Tomb (1628), in Agra, India.

distinctive western Islamic style. This included such features as domed mosques with minarets, and calm prayer halls decorated with colored tiles arranged in intricate geometric patterns.

By the time Cimabue and Duccio were at work in Italy, Islamic artists had created some of the most sumptuous and ornate buildings in the world. In about 960–976 AD, for instance, the Great Mosque in Córdoba, Spain, was decorated with a domed ceiling, covered inside with glittering mosaics in gold and blue.

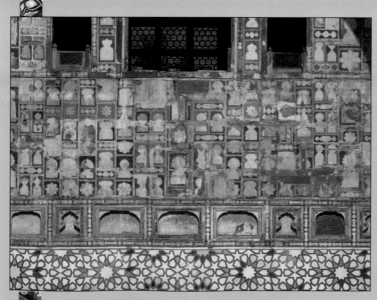

Wall decoration at Sikandra, north of Agra, showing the inventive variety of Islamic patterns.

Oil Painting in Northern Europe

In the cold and the damp of northern Europe, paintings made using the fresco and tempera techniques deteriorated rapidly. In around 1400, however, a new kind of paint was developed, using pigments mixed with oil. The paint was slow to dry, but created a lasting surface. This "oil paint" was thick and colorful, producing effects rather like manuscript illuminations. Also, colors could be blended on the painting itself to create smooth changes in tone. This made it easier for the artist to create rich shadow, and to build up shapes that looked three-dimensional.

Pioneers of Oil Painting

It is said that the inventor of oil painting was the painter Jan van Eyck (c.1390–1441). He was from Flanders (an area that included parts of modern day France, Belgium, and Holland), and was court painter to Philip the Good, the Duke of Burgundy, in Bruges (now in Belgium). It is more likely that he learned the technique from someone else, but he was certainly one of the first painters to show what extraordinary and rich effects could be achieved with oil paint.

Van Eyck also shows a passion for tiny detail, such as the embroidery on clothes, even the patterns in the tiles on the floor. His most celebrated work is the giant altarpiece in Ghent, Belgium, called *The Adoration of the Mystic Lamb*, painted with his brother Hubert. It consists of 12 color panels containing 280 figures.

Angel Concert, a panel from Jan and Hubert van Eyck's Adoration of the Mystic Lamb (1432), in Ghent Cathedral.

The technique of oil painting was used by many Flemish painters, such as Hugo van der Goes (1440–1482). At this time, a great deal of trade passed between the cities of Flanders and Italy. Hugo van der Goes's most celebrated work is the *Portinari Altarpiece*, in Florence. It is an indication of how Flemish oil painting was appreciated in Italy. Meanwhile, an Italian artist called Antonello da Messina (c.1430–1479) learned about oil painting, perhaps from Flemish artists in Naples or Milan, and took the idea to Venice.

The Adoration of the Shepherds, the central Nativity scene from the Portinari Altarpiece (c.1476), by Hugo van der Goes.

Around the World
China

Using their tiny brushes and smooth paints, European oil painters and manuscript illuminators were able to depict plants and flowers and other features of the natural world in remarkably fine detail. In China, from as early as the 900s, artists were also painting from nature. But the outcome was very different.

Bird and Ripening Apple, painted on silk during the Song Period (960–1279) in China. Artists of this period specialized in small-scale, intimate scenes from nature.

Fleeting Moments of Beauty

Chinese artists captured the details of nature, but they also injected a sense of life into their work. The bird in the picture looks as though it might burst into song at any moment. This effect was achieved by careful observation. They could also work quickly, using soft brushes and water-based colors, painted on sheets of silk or paper. Chinese artists created realistic but poetic scenes, which reflected a religious celebration of the simple beauty of nature.

Early Renaissance Sculpture

In the 1400s, Florence, in Italy, developed as a center for art and architecture. In 1401, a competition was launched to decorate the doors of the baptistery for the cathedral. Lorenzo Ghiberti (1378–1455) won and designed the doors with a series of magnificent panels in bronze. The architecture shown in the background of these pictures was Greek or Roman. Architects were copying Roman models to build Christian churches and cathedrals. Some people called Florence the "New Rome."

One of the ten gilded-bronze panels "Gates of Paradise" (1424–1452), by Lorenzo Ghiberti for the doors of the Baptistery of Florence.

Roman Models

One of Ghiberti's pupils was Donato di Niccolo, better known as Donatello (1386–1466), who trained with him from 1404 to 1407. Donatello no doubt helped in Ghiberti's busy workshop, producing the baptistery doors, but he soon demonstrated his individuality in work of great emotional force. He sculpted in wood, marble, and bronze, showing a gift for natural expression and lifelike proportions and posture. In about 1430, Donatello went to Rome to study the sculpture of the ancient Romans and Greeks. He realized that it was far better than anything produced in medieval times.

The experience set a new challenge for him, and after this his work changed and became more assured. His *David* was the first free-standing nude statue created since Roman times. Some have even argued that it is not David with the head of Goliath, from the biblical story, but the Roman god Mercury, with the head of Argus. From 1443 to 1453, Donatello was in Padua, working on a lifesize statue of the warrior Gattamelata on horseback— again, the first such monument since Roman times.

Mary Magdalene (c.1455), a painted and gilded wood sculpture by Donatello.

Around the World
Africa

Bronze statues are made by a process called "casting." First, a model is made, usually in clay or wax, and this is then pressed into a mold. Then molten (liquid) bronze is poured into the empty mold. This ancient craft was widely practiced, but only in some places was it used to create art. One of these places was West Africa.

Faces of the Past

Bronze-casting was perfected at several centers in West Africa as early as the 800s or 900s. From the 900s, the sculptors of Ife, in Nigeria, were producing masks and heads cast in brass and copper, created to look like realistic portraits. Europeans knew little about this work until after 1470, when the first Portuguese merchants and explorers began slowly to explore the coast of West Africa.

A copper head from Ife, Nigeria (1100s–1400s).

Donatello's interest in Roman sculpture had a carry-over effect in painting. Very little ancient Roman painting survived, but Renaissance artists were inspired by the real-life, three-dimensional qualities of Roman sculpture to improve their figure painting.

Florence was dominated by wealthy families, and by the 1430s the most important was the family of merchants and bankers called the Medicis. Keen to display their good taste and wealth, as well as their power, the Medicis became important patrons of the arts. It is said that Donatello's *David* was used as the centerpiece at the wedding of Lorenzo de' Medici.

Bust of a Youth with a Medallion at His Neck, a Roman-style bronze sculpture, believed to be by Donatello.

Perspective

European artists of the Renaissance set themselves the task of representing the world around them as realistically as possible. They wanted the scenes they painted to look just like part of the real world, as you might see it with your own eyes. In fact, this is a trick. Paintings are painted on flat surfaces, in two dimensions. Reality is in three dimensions: it recedes (goes back) into the distance and has "depth." To make their trick convincing, artists had to master the art of perspective.

The Tribute Money (c.1425), by Masaccio.

Near and Far

When Ghiberti won the competition to decorate the doors of the Baptistery in Florence, one of the other contestants was Filippo Brunelleschi (1377–1446). It is said that he gave up sculpture after this disappointment and concentrated on architecture. His great triumph was the splendid dome of the Florence Cathedral, built 1420–1436. Like many gifted artists in the Renaissance, he had

many talents, and was not just an architect and sculptor, but also a painter. He is said to be the person who discovered the way perspective works—the way in which parallel lines in a building all lead to a single vanishing point. His ideas were put into practice by the Italian painter Tommaso di Ser Giovanni di Mone Cassai, known as Masaccio (1401–1428), whose mastery of the technique can be seen, for example, in the buildings in The Tribute Money.

16

The Naming of John the Baptist (c.1434), by Fra Angelico.

Perspective was considered the key to making painted scenes look real. It was quickly adopted by all the leading Italian painters of the time, such as Fra Angelico (c.1395–1455), Piero della Francesca (c.1415–1492), and Andrea Mantegna (c.1430–1506). In fact, mastery of perspective seemed so important that some artists allowed architectural elements to take over their paintings. This can be seen in Piero della Francesca's mysterious *Flagellation of Christ*, where the main subject, believed to be Christ, is almost lost in his perfectly painted surroundings.

However, perspective is not simply a question of lining up the buildings correctly. It is also about creating a convincing sense of depth.

Masaccio was really a nickname meaning something like "dolt" or "sloppy." He was so devoted to painting that he took no care of himself or his looks.

This is achieved by showing the way that color alters as distance from the viewer increases. Distance also alters the color tones and shadows in crowds, even in faces seen close up. The depiction of shadow to give a convincing three-dimensional effect called "modeling" was the next great technical challenge in creating the illusion of depth.

The Vanishing Point

Brunelleschi discovered that all parallel lines in a picture—such as buildings, or furniture—point to a single vanishing point. This was not fully appreciated until his time, as witnessed, for example, in Cimabue's throne on page 9. Pictures can have more than one vanishing point if, for example, buildings or furniture are set at an angle. It would have helped Giotto to know this when he painted the hut on page 9. Brunelleschi's discovery made it much easier for artists to create a realistic illusion of depth.

Vanishing point

The Flagellation of Christ (c.1450), by Piero della Francesca. The parallel elements of the buildings—roof lines, columns, paving stones—all line up to a single vanishing point.

Nonreligious Art

During the Renaissance, Italy was divided into a large number of small states which were usually ruled by a major city, such as Florence, Urbino, or Venice. These "city states" were governed by wealthy, powerful families, who prided themselves on the fine quality of their buildings, paintings, sculpture, music, and education. They had the money to pay the best artists to make portraits of themselves, their wives, and their children. Artists still did a lot of work for the Church, but now they did not depend on the Church alone to make a living.

Around the World
Mayan art

A series of great civilizations developed in Mexico and Central America from about 2000 BC–Olmec, Maya, and Aztec. They had no contact with the rest of the world until the Spanish arrived in the early 1500s. Their art bears little resemblance to the painting and sculpture of either Europe or Asia.

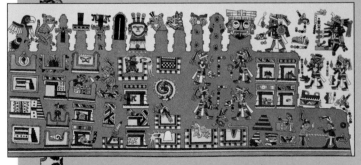

Mayan picture writing, recording the deeds of gods and divine rulers.

History in Art

The Mayan civilization was at its height from about the 500s to 800s. Their art was mainly concerned with recording the deeds of their rulers. They used picture writing, showing highly stylized, blocklike figures either facing sideways or face on. They were not trying to paint realistic images.

18

Real People in the Real World

A similar development took place all over Europe, wherever there were wealthy rulers and a rich merchant class who wanted to commission paintings done especially for them. Jan van Eyck, for instance, worked for the Duke of Burgundy, who ruled over prosperous land covering eastern France, Belgium, and The Netherlands. In 1434, he painted the famous double portrait of an Italian banker working in Bruges, Giovanni Arnolfini, and his bride, Giovanna Cenami. Like many paintings of the day, it is full of symbols, which viewers of the time would immediately have understood. The dog, for example, is a symbol of loyalty in love.

Virgin and Child with Chancellor Rolin (c.1430), by Jan van Eyck.

The Church still played a powerful role in the lives of all Europeans, and many portraits underlined the piety (religious devotion) of the sitter. Nicholas Rolin, chancellor to the Duke of Burgundy, even commissioned Jan van Eyck to paint a portrait of himself in the presence of the Madonna and Child.

The detail in the painting shows van Eyck's fascination for making accurate images of everything around him. This new sense of wonder and questioning about the world was typical of the Renaissance. Artists looked, observed, and studied their subjects, and painted what they saw with a new kind of honesty and directness. Some portraits were so honest they were not flattering at all.

The Arnolfini Marriage (1434), by Jan van Eyck, depicting the wealthy Italian merchant Giovanni Arnolfini and his young wife in their home in Bruges.

Classical Subjects

During the Renaissance, artists and scholars rediscovered many of the myths and legends of ancient, or classical, Greece and Rome. They were fascinated to find a complex system of beliefs and wonderful stories that had nothing to do with the Bible and Christianity. Some painters decided to make these stories into pictures. The most famous was the Italian Sandro Botticelli (1445–1510).

Pagan Images

Botticelli's name was Alessandro di Mariano Filipepi, but he was known by his nickname, meaning "little barrel." Compared to works by earlier Italians such as Masaccio, Botticelli's paintings seem more relaxed. He was less concerned with reproducing the real world. Instead, he wanted to conjure up the world of myth and imagination, and painted with a new kind of freshness which mirrored the youthful spirit of the Renaissance.

Two of Botticelli's most famous paintings, *La Primavera* (a mythical depiction of spring) and *The Birth of Venus*, represented a major break from the tradition of religious paintings: not only were they on classical, non-Christian themes, they were also large. They reflect

La Primavera, or Spring (c.1478), by Botticelli.

the great Renaissance interest in classical philosophy, and suggest the kinds of discussions people had on subjects such as the meaning of beauty.

Botticelli was very successful at the height of his career. But soon his style seemed old fashioned. Another painter working in Florence had brought a new sophistication to painting. His name was Leonardo da Vinci.

Leonardo da Vinci

With great advances in painting, sculpture, science, and architecture, the world of art and learning entered a period known as the High Renaissance, which lasted from about 1500 to 1520. It was the result of work produced by a number of people with an exceptional range of talents. One of the greatest was the Italian Leonardo da Vinci (1452–1519)—painter, sculptor, architect, engineer, mathematician, scientist, and philosopher.

The Smile of Genius

Born near the town of Vinci, Leonardo started serving as an apprentice at the studio of an older artist. Part of the training involved the study of engineering and mechanics. Leonardo's teacher was Andrea del Verrocchio (c.1435–1488), who was so amazed at the talent of the young Leonardo that he gave up painting! Leonardo stayed in Florence until he was about 30, painting portraits and religious paintings. Then he moved to Milan, to work as "painter and engineer" to Duke Ludovico Sforza.

During these years, Leonardo perfected his oil-painting technique. This can be seen in the *Mona Lisa*, perhaps his best-known painting. Few previous paintings had shown such a lifelike, natural look. The portrait catches a

The Mona Lisa (c.1503), now in the Louvre, Paris.

flickering smile that lasted just a moment. The shading creates a rounded, convincing three-dimensional effect, contrasted with the hazy landscape in the background. The painting remains a mystery: it is said to be a portrait of the wife of Francesco del Giocondo, a wealthy man from Florence.

21

From an early age, Leonardo had loved to draw from nature. He sketched and observed, making studies of plants and animals.

In fact, much to the frustration of his patrons, he painted only about 25 pictures. These are mainly portraits of people at the court of Duke Ludovico Sforza, noted for their careful

The Lady with the Ermine (c.1490), a portrait of Cecilia Gallerani by Leonardo.

composition and great tenderness. Leonardo was extraordinarily gifted, but he had problems finishing the paintings he started and could not resist the temptation to experiment. When in Milan, he painted his famous mural, *The Last Supper* (c.1495). He tried out a new technique for painting on walls. As a result, the painting started deteriorating even in his lifetime, and has been restored countless times since.

Sfumato

Leonardo brought a new delicacy to oil painting, which was still fairly new in Italy. One of the ways he achieved this was a technique known as sfumato, from an Italian word meaning shaded, or hazy, as if seen through mist or smoke.

Leonardo observed that in nature, objects do not have hard lines around them. Instead, their colors shade gently to the edge, and often merge into the shading of neighboring objects "without lines or borders," as Leonardo himself put it, "in the manner of smoke." This can be seen, for example, in the shadowy areas in the figures of *St. Anne with Mary and the Child Jesus.*

Leonardo's St. Anne with Mary and the Child Jesus, completed in about 1510.

Renaissance Man

In Milan, Leonardo was also employed as an architect and engineer, and spent much of his time designing canals, fortifications, and weapons. Using his fertile imagination, he also toyed with new ideas, drawing designs for multibarreled guns, flying machines, a parachute, and a tank—inventions that were turned into reality only some 400 years later.

He also continued his scientific studies. By dissecting dead bodies, he carried out detailed research into human anatomy. He filled thousands of pages of large notebooks with sketches, diagrams, and notes written backward in mirror writing—he found this easier because he was left-handed.

A giant bronze statue of a horse designed by Leonardo in about 1490 was made 500 years later. Erected in Milan in 1999, it stands 23 feet high and weighs 13 tons.

In Milan, Leonardo was also asked to make sculpture. Once again, he brought a mixture of intense observation and experimentation to the task. His most ambitious work was to design a vast bronze sculpture of Duke Ludovico Sforza's father on horseback. Unfortunately, Milan came under threat of war from France, and the bronze was melted to make cannons.

Milan fell to the French in 1499, and Leonardo went to Mantua and Venice before returning to Florence. In 1506, he was invited back to Milan by the French governor. Now in the pay of the French king, he devoted most of his time to his scientific studies. War forced him to move again in 1513, this time to Rome. But three years later, he was invited by King François I of France to live near his palace at Amboise, on the Loire River in France. Leonardo spent the last three years of his life there and died at the age of 67.

Right: Bronze statuette of a man on horseback, based on Leonardo's designs for the Sforza statue.

Top: Leonardo's famous study of human proportions, drawn in ink (c 1487).

Bottom: Design for a mechanical catapult (c.1490).

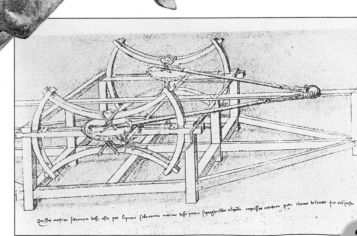

The Spread of the Italian Renaissance

Many of the early achievements of the Renaissance took place in Italy. But European kings, nobles, and merchants were keen to join the trend. While François I invited Leonardo to France, many of the artists of northern Europe traveled to Italy, returning home with new skills they had learned. The

German artist Albrecht Dürer (1471–1528), for example, traveled to Italy in 1494 and again in 1505–1507. By this time, many of the ideas of the Renaissance had spread across Europe, largely because of the development of printing.

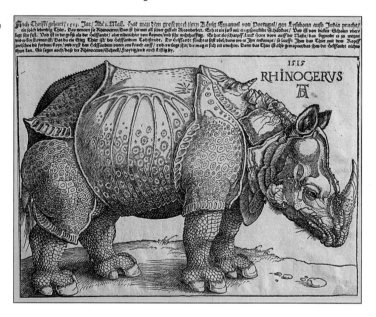

Woodcut print of a rhinoceros (1515), by Dürer.

Mass-produced Art

The art of printing, mainly from woodcuts, dates back many centuries. The first known printed book was made in China in 868 AD. But in about 1440, German Johannes Gutenberg made a major breakthrough. He found a way of mass-producing individual letters (or "movable type") with which books could be printed. This revolutionized book production. Now, instead of being laboriously hand-copied by monks, books could be printed rapidly and in large numbers.

Albrecht Dürer was one of the first great artists to take full advantage of this invention. As a young man, he trained with a leading book illustrator in Nuremberg, Germany, learning to make woodcuts and engravings.

Book illustration occupied much of his career, during which he ran a busy workshop in Nuremberg. Many of his prints show his highly original style: very detailed, brilliantly drawn, full of energy, and with touches of humor. Throughout his life, he was fascinated by proportion—getting the sizes of faces, bodies, and things correct in relation to each other. He was also a superb painter, as demonstrated by his *Self-portrait* of 1500. But he was best known for his prints, because many copies of his work could be made and sold all over Europe.

When the Reformation caused turmoil in Basel, Holbein moved. With a letter of introduction from Erasmus, he went to England to work for Sir Thomas More, who later became chancellor to King Henry VIII. From 1536, Holbein worked at the court of Henry VIII, painting his portrait a number of times. One of his tasks was to travel abroad to paint portraits of women that Henry considered marrying. He painted Anne of Cleves, Henry's fourth bride, and made her look quite attractive, but when Henry saw her in the flesh he was disappointed, and the marriage was a disaster. Holbein was not blamed, however, and he continued painting for Henry. He died in London, aged about 46.

Portrait Painter to the Famous

Another talented artist from Germany was Hans Holbein the Younger (1497–1543), the son of the painter Hans Holbein the Elder (c.1465–1534). He lived in Basel, Switzerland, often working alongside his father. When he was about 20, he crossed the Alps to Italy, and returned with a much softer style.

He decorated houses with his paintings and, like Dürer, made prints, but soon he was best known for his portraits. He was often asked to paint famous people, such as the Dutch scholar Desiderius Erasmus, one of the great figures of Renaissance learning, who was living in Basel in the 1520s.

Portrait of Erasmus of Rotterdam, who was a critic of the Church. Painted by Hans Holbein the Younger in 1523.

Figures in a Landscape

Almost all paintings in European art during the medieval and Renaissance periods focus on people. Landscape appears only in the background. It may sometimes be detailed and beautifully painted, yet it remains secondary to the main focus of the painting. But the attitude toward landscape was changing. Gradually, the landscape was becoming not just a background, but part of the main composition. A good example of this is the Pietà by Giovanni Bellini (c.1431–1516), one of the leading artists of the Italian city of Venice.

Scenery as a Subject

Behind Bellini's tragic scene (above) of Mary holding her dead son on her knee, is a detailed picture of an Italian landscape as it appeared in his own time. There is a message in this: although Christ died 1,500 years before, he and his teachings live on in the modern world. The paintings of Bellini's gifted pupil Giorgione (c.1477–1510) take this idea one stage further. In a painting like *The Three Philosophers*, the figures are not only set in a lifelike landscape, they interact with it. Giorgione was also held in regard because his paintings evoke a powerful sense of mood.

But Giorgione's main subject was still the figures, not the landscape. Very few artists painted landscape for its own sake. Albrecht Dürer was an exception: he painted

Hunters in the Snow (1565), by Pieter Brueghel the Elder.

watercolor sketches of landscapes without figures, notably in the Alps and around his hometown. It seems that they were simply for his own private record. In many of the works of the later Flemish painter Pieter Brueghel the Elder (c.1525–1569), the figures are still the main focus, but they are seen as part of a landscape, as in *Hunters in the Snow*, one of a series illustrating the months of the year.

Around the World
Japan

Much Japanese culture was influenced by its great neighbor, China. The Japanese borrowed Chinese writing, religion, and styles of art, but they adapted each to create their own unique culture. There was no contact with European culture until 1543.

Landscape for Its Own Sake

Like the Chinese, the Japanese had a deep respect for nature. Artists tried to capture not only the natural beauty of landscape, but also its moods in changing weather conditions. Here, the hills and houses are almost obscured by a morning mist. There are no people—the landscape itself is the subject.

Japanese landscape on a scroll in the Muromachi period (c.1333–1568).

Brueghel was unusual. He was born in Flanders, the home of Jan van Eyck. He traveled to Italy in the 1550s, but there is very little evidence of this in his work. Like Dürer, he made sketches of the Alps, which seem to have impressed him more than anything else he saw on his journey.

When he returned home, he made a series of landscape prints. He also used his own highly individual, slightly naïve (childlike) style to paint scenes from the rural life of Flanders. He often placed biblical stories in this setting, just as Bellini placed the *Pietà* in Italy. A famous example is his *Massacre of the Innocents*, making a snow-covered Flemish village the backdrop for the horrific violence of the Bible story where Herod slaughters children after the birth of Christ.

The Three Philosophers (c.1508), by Giorgione.
The seated figure is making a study of the landscape.

27

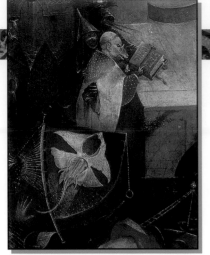

The World of the Imagination

Renaissance artists struggled to find ways to depict the real world as accurately as possible. But they realized that they could also conjure up images taken entirely from the imagination. They used new painting skills, made possible by oil paints and by close observation of nature, to produce strange and grotesque fantasies. Many of these were based on old religious ideas, such as that of hell, and were perhaps also influenced by distortions of the mind, such as nightmares.

Weird and Wonderful

Some artists are known only for their grotesquely imaginative work. Most famous of all is the Dutch artist Hieronymus Bosch (1450–1516). He painted images of mutant beasts, monsters, demons, and demented humans torturing each other in unspeakable ways. All his paintings have a religious message, showing, for instance, the horrors that sinners face after death. However, there is also an enthusiastic, playful relish in these images, and some are humorous.

The story of St. Antony had a particular fascination for many artists: he was an early Christian saint and hermit who lived a very strict life in the desert of Egypt, suffering all kinds of hallucinations. The German painter Matthias Grünewald (c.1470–1528) painted The Temptation of St. Antony using the full power of his imagination.

Demons, from The Temptation of St. Antony (1513), by Matthias Grünewald.

The Market Gardener (1590), by Giuseppe Arcimboldo. This seems an odd title for a bowl of vegetables, until you turn the picture upside down.

The Italian painter Giuseppe Arcimboldo (1527–1593) took fantasy in quite a different direction. He is best known for his pictures of faces composed entirely out of food—usually fruit or vegetables, sometimes fish—all beautifully painted. The result is fascinating, funny, and grotesque all at once.

All these fantasy paintings are, in their way, the opposite of the Renaissance ideal, which was based on learning, observation, and reason.

Around the World
Himalayas

High in the Himalayan Mountains lived monks who practiced Buddhism. Some painted complex pictures of the Buddha and scenes from the scriptures, filled with gods, animals, patterns, and symbols. Some images were painted on monastery walls. Others, called tankas, were painted on cloth, which could be rolled up.

A Different Reality

These paintings of the spirit world look like products of the imagination. But Buddhist monks argue otherwise. They say that this is reality, what the gods really look like, as witnessed by monks after very long periods of meditation.

Buddhist painting at Tikse Monastery in Ladakh, northern India.

Raphael

In about 1500, the focus of the Italian Renaissance switched from Florence and Milan to Rome. This is because a powerful and wealthy set of popes had come to power, and wanted to make the Vatican, their headquarters in Rome, into a glittering symbol of the power of the Church. One of these popes was Julius II, who was elected in 1503. He invited the best artists of the day to decorate his palace. This included the painter and architect Raffaello Sanzio, also known as Raphael (1483–1520).

Calm Beauty

Raphael was from Urbino. He was a skilled portraitist and worked in Florence from 1504 to 1508, where he learned much from great artists such as Leonardo da Vinci and Michelangelo. He specialized in religious paintings. The clarity, gracefulness, and softness of touch in his work conveys a sense of deep spiritual holiness and calm. In 1508, he was called to Rome and commissioned to decorate a room in the Vatican called the Stanza della Segnatura with a series of four large frescoes.

Raphael took on an ambitious task: to show the aspects of Renaissance learning and to display the link between Christianity and the wisdom of ancient Greece and Rome. In *The School of Athens* he shows the great philosophers of ancient Greece, centering

The School of Athens (1508–1511), by Raphael.

upon Plato and Aristotle and surrounded by magnificent classical architecture. All are shown in perfect perspective. Raphael remained in Rome, designing part of St. Peter's Basilica, the great church of the Vatican. His early death at 37 caused widespread grief. He was considered then—and for centuries afterward—Europe's greatest painter ever.

Michelangelo

Michelangelo Buonarroti, known simply as Michelangelo (1475–1564), was also working in Rome at this time. While Raphael was friendly, kind, and relaxed, Michelangelo was messy, arrogant, and utterly absorbed in his work. Brought up in the court of Florence, with Lorenzo de' Medici as his patron, Michelangelo learned the art of fresco painting first, then switched to sculpture. He moved to Rome in 1496, where he studied ancient Roman sculpture. He quickly established a reputation as one of the greatest sculptors the world has ever known.

Michelangelo the Sculptor

This reputation was largely based on his first *Pietà* (below), a piece of exceptional grace and tenderness. The word Pietà comes from the Italian word for pity. A Pietà is a painting or sculpture of the Virgin Mary holding the dead Christ on her lap. The naturalistic poses of Michelangelo's figures in his *Pietà*, and the details of the clothes and skin, show an extraordinary ability to convert marble into something dazzlingly lifelike. As was typical of Michelangelo's work, however, this piece caused some angry disputes. Some people argued that it showed disrespect to the Christian story, because Mary, mother of Jesus, is portrayed as a young woman.

Disputes apart, it was a remarkable work for a sculptor still in his mid-twenties. He left Rome in 1501, and returned to Florence in triumph.

The Pietà (1498–1499), sculpted when Michelangelo was just 25 years old, and now in St. Peter's Basilica, Vatican City.

Moses, sculpted by Michelangelo in 1513–1515 and 1542 for the tomb of Pope Julius II in the Church of St. Peter in Chains, Rome.

David was carved from a slab of marble found lying in the workshops of Florence Cathedral. It had been left by another sculptor 40 years before.

David, sculpted in Florence 1501–1504.

David

It was during this period that Michelangelo created one of his most famous works, his large, marble statue, *David*. Standing more than thirteen feet high, it shows Michelangelo's great knowledge and understanding of anatomy and human proportion. It has all the skill of a work from ancient Rome, plus all the relaxed self-confidence of the Renaissance.

Michelangelo returned to Rome in 1505, called by Pope Julius II to create a sculpture for his elaborate tomb. Michelangelo eventually worked on his statue of *Moses* for the tomb after Julius's death in 1513, and the project dragged out for another 30 years. The main reason for the delay was that Michelangelo was also asked to carry out one of the most ambitious projects of the entire Renaissance: painting the ceiling of the Vatican's Sistine Chapel.

Sculpting from Marble

Michelangelo is said to have worked for 20 hours a day, for three years, carving *David* from a block of marble. Before starting on the marble, though, he had made a small plaster model of the finished figure. He used this to make full-scale wax and clay copies of the limbs, which served as guides as he hammered and chiseled at the marble block. First he produced the rough shape of the statue, then he used finer chisels to do more delicate shaping, ending up with needle-thin chisels for the fine features, such as the mouth and eyes. Finally, the marble surface was smoothed and polished.

Japan

Although strongly influenced by China, by the 1100s Japan had begun to develop its own style of art. Attempts to invade Japan by the Mongol rulers of China were thwarted in 1274 and 1281. This gave the Japanese a sense that their nation had heavenly protection, and in the years that followed, Japan consciously developed many aspects of its culture, including Zen Buddhism.

Sculpture in Wood

The Japanese had developed highly sophisticated techniques of wood carving from at least the 600s. They tended to use wood, and also clay, because there was little suitable stone in Japan. They made lifesize sculptures of their Buddhist deities (gods), which were often elaborately painted. The religious statues followed old traditions that gave each of their deities certain characteristic features. For instance, the "enlightened one," Jizo Bosatsu, savior of souls in hell, is shown dressed as a priest, with an enlarged head and a face of serene calm.

By contrast, portrait sculptures representing historic figures are often exceptionally realistic. The Zen Buddhists excelled in this kind of sculpture. They would make full-size, strikingly realistic portraits of their great teachers or founders of the monasteries, usually not while they were living, but as a memorial after they had died.

Sculpture in wood of the Buddhist divinity, Jizo Bosatsu, Muromachi period (1333—1568).

Michelangelo as a Painter

Michelangelo was not keen on the Sistine Chapel project: gifted though he was as a painter, he considered himself a sculptor. In fact, Michelangelo used paint rather as if he was sculpting. The figures in his *Holy Family* look muscular and three-dimensional, with little of the soft shading and delicacy of Leonardo or Raphael.

Julius II was persuasive, and Michelangelo began work on the Sistine Chapel ceiling in 1508, just as Raphael was beginning work nearby on the Stanza della Segnatura. To the frustration of Julius II, Michelangelo worked for more than four years, refusing to hurry or take on assistants.

It was a huge task. Over an area measuring 131 by 39 feet—the size of a tennis court—Michelangelo undertook to illustrate a dozen scenes from the Bible. These included the hand of God giving life to Adam through the tip of his finger, plus portraits of the Prophets and Sibyls who foretold the birth of Christ. This complex scheme was linked together by artificial architectural elements, painted three-dimensionally to look real. On completion of the Sistine Chapel ceiling in 1512, Michelangelo was 37 years old.

The Holy Family (c.1504), by Michelangelo, painted in tempera on wood.

Above: The Sistine Chapel (ceiling, 1508–1512), looking west toward the Last Judgment (1536–1541).

Right: The Prophet Zacharias (1509), from the Sistine Chapel.

The Last Judgment

He now returned to work on the tomb of Julius II, but was soon commissioned by the new pope, Leo X (Giovanni de' Medici), to try his hand at architecture, starting with churches in Florence. He returned to Rome in 1534, now to work for another pope, Paul III (Alessandro Farnese), and began work on a huge new painting in the Sistine Chapel, this time on the west wall. He chose as his subject the *Last Judgment*—a vision of the end of the world.

After Michelangelo's death, loincloths were painted onto the naked figures of the Sistine Chapel. The nude figures were considered indecent.

By this time, the ideals of the Renaissance had begun to lose their luster. Rome had been sacked and vandalized by the troops of Emperor Charles V in 1527, as war raged across Europe.

It was against this depressing background that Michelangelo painted his *Last Judgment*, which took him five years (1536–1541) to complete. It is a dark and disturbing work, much more somber than his earlier ceiling.

For the last years of his long life, Michelangelo devoted himself to architecture, taking over the building of St. Peter's Basilica in 1546. But the project remained uncompleted at his death in 1564, at the considerable age of 88.

Mannerism and the Counter-Reformation

In his paintings, Michelangelo depicted muscular people dressed in bright clothes and filled with intense emotion. This kind of exaggeration became one of the key elements of "Mannerism." The Mannerists no longer simply copied what they saw, they exaggerated reality with distorted natural shapes. This was seen as a way of expressing energy and movement, and of injecting their own emotions and a feeling of unearthly spirituality into their work.

Abandoning the Renaissance

The Reformation, which resulted in the formation of Protestantism, was a crisis for the Christian Church. Roman Catholics fought back with the Counter-Reformation and many people blamed the Renaissance for the troubles. It had encouraged people to reason and use observation, but it had led them to question the Catholic Church. They decided that the Renaissance had led to Protestantism.

The Catholic Church wanted a new kind of art to express the spirituality and emotion of Catholicism, so it encouraged Mannerism. The movement lasted from about 1520 to 1600.

The word "mannerism" comes from the Italian "maniera," meaning "style." It was this emphasis on style that set the Mannerists apart. This is seen best of all in the work of Parmigianino (1503–1540; real name: Girolamo Francesco Mazzola), who gave to his figures a stretched look.

Madonna with the Long Neck (c.1535), by Parmigianino.

The Light of Christ

The Mannerists were among the best painters of a new generation of artists. Pontormo (1494–1556; real name: Jacopo Carrucci), for instance, was taught by Leonardo da Vinci, among others. He is known above all for his highly-charged religious painting, his dynamic compositions and his use of strongly contrasting colors. *Supper at Emmaus* shows Christ newly risen from the dead and joining two disciples at supper. The action is static, but the composition is full of movement—leading the eye around all the faces, but always back to Christ in the middle. This painting was famous enough to merit a very precise copy by Jacopo Chimenti da Empoli more than 50 years after the original was made.

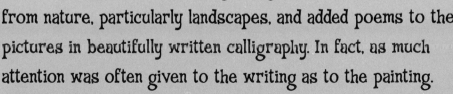

Around the World
China

The long-lasting Ming dynasty (1368–1644) in China followed the expulsion of the Mongols and ushered in a period of stability. Many of the painters painted from nature, particularly landscapes, and added poems to the pictures in beautifully written calligraphy. In fact, as much attention was often given to the writing as to the painting.

The Poetry of Nature

As with the Mannerists on the other side of the world, the work of these poet-painters was gradually becoming more stylized. They focused on shapes found in nature, assembling them to create a feeling of breathtaking grandeur. Composition was carefully contrived—but it also had to look entirely natural.

A mountain landscape drawn in ink by the poet and painter T'ang Yin (1470–1524).

Venice

While the Mannerists became fashionable in the rest of Italy, the city of Venice followed a rather different course. Venice was built on islands in a lagoon, just off the coast of northeast Italy. The Venetians created a powerful trading empire, dominating the trade of the eastern Mediterranean. This meant that Venice had many rich merchants to buy paintings. But the damp conditions of this city of canals meant that fresco and tempera were unsuitable. Venice, therefore, took to painting in oil on canvas, and excelled in it from the days of Giovanni Bellini (c.1431–1516) onward.

Titian

Oil painting skills were passed on through a series of technically brilliant artists, such as Bellini's pupils, Giorgione (c.1477–1510) and Titian (c.1488–1576), and later continued by Veronese (c.1528–1588).

Danaë (1545–1546), a scene from Greek mythology by Titian.

Titian (real name Tiziano Vecellio) was the leading painter in Venice for 60 years following the death of Bellini in 1516. He painted richly colored canvases, often depicting classical myths, and maintaining the Renaissance tradition of painting nudes. *Danaë*, for instance, shows the story from the Greek myth in which the god Jupiter, who loves Danaë, takes the form of a shower of gold to visit her in her prisonlike tower. But Titian also painted a large number of works for churches, such as his famous *Assumption of the Virgin*. The three-tiered composition shows the Virgin Mary rising above the Apostles toward God in heaven.

It is full of the energy and movement which Titian injected into his painting, supported by his superb technical abilities. Titian was one of the first artists to apply oil paint with expression—to use the brushstrokes themselves to convey emotion. He was reported to use his fingers as much as a brush when he put the final touches to a painting.

Titian's Assumption of the Virgin (1516–1518). This altarpiece for the Church of Santa Maria dei Frari in Venice measures nearly 23 feet high, the largest work completed by Titian.

Sumptuous Beauty

Veronese (real name: Paolo Caliari) became known for his superb technique and his ability to create enormous compositions. He used these to decorate the walls and ceilings of palaces (such as the Doge's Palace in Venice) and churches. In his paintings he liked to create a sumptuous world of wealthy courtiers, musicians, feasting guests, and entertainers, all of whom appear natural, lifelike, and energetic. Veronese was also famous for his ability to paint clothes.

Detail from The Triumph of Nemesis over the Sins (c.1555), by Veronese.

He especially favored the rich, bejeweled silks of women, using a palette of bright colors highlighted with white. In fact, he painted religious scenes with such sumptuous richness that he ran into trouble with the Church. He was also a master of a skill called foreshortening. This is used especially on ceilings to give the impression that the figures really are standing above the viewer, with their heads closer to the sky.

Tintoretto and El Greco

Working alongside Veronese in the Doge's Palace was a pupil of Titian called Jacopo Robusti, known as Tintoretto (1519–1594) because his father was a dyer (a "tinter" of cloth). His work has the skill and richness typical of the Venetian painters, but unlike them, he adopted a Mannerist style. His paintings are full of drama, with rapid brushwork, color contrasts, movement, and bright lighting effects. Meanwhile a painter in Spain was taking the Mannerist style to a new extreme. Because of his origins, he was known simply as El Greco, "the Greek" (1541–1614).

The Image of Faith

The unusual lighting in Tintoretto's paintings was the result of a technique he used. He painted from wax models of his figures, lit with a bright light. Like Veronese, Tintoretto painted interiors, decorating entire rooms with his work. He decorated most of the interior of the Scuola di San Rocca, one of the wealthy, semireligious professional guilds in Venice.

At this time, the Greek island of Crete was part of the Venetian empire. In about 1567, a gifted Cretan artist called Doménikos Theotokópoulos traveled to Venice and became an enthusiastic admirer of Tintoretto's work. A few years later, he traveled to Rome and studied the paintings of Michelangelo. Then in 1577, he went to the city of Toledo, in Spain, to paint an altarpiece. He remained there for the rest of his life, becoming known as El Greco.

El Greco's Annunciation, illustrating the moment when the Virgin Mary was told by the Angel Gabriel that she would be the mother of Christ.

Around the World
Mexico

Until the 1400s, Europeans knew very little about the world beyond their own continent. Searching for a trade route to the Far East, the Italian navigator Christopher Columbus, stumbled upon the Americas in 1492. By 1522, Ferdinand Magellan's expedition had sailed right around the world. Suddenly the world had opened up to Europe.

An artist's impression of the first meeting between Cortés and the Aztec emperor Montezuma in 1519.

Explorers and Conquerors

This was also a turning point in the history of world art. The Europeans wanted knowledge, wealth, and land, and they set out to claim the world for themselves. This had particularly harsh consequences in Mexico and Central America, for example, where the Aztec empire was swiftly demolished by the Spanish, led by Hernán Cortés, in 1521–1526. Gradually, European countries came to dominate much of the world and to influence world culture.

El Greco's work was really like no other at the time. He made no attempt to paint the real world around him. Instead he painted religious subjects charged with emotional intensity. To achieve this, he used exaggerated human shapes, rapid brush strokes, and a palette of simple, pale colors. As a result, his paintings feel as though they are charged with a kind of electricity. The backgrounds are sketchy, and his figures seem to float in the space created for them. It is as though he is portraying the world of faith, something altogether more invigorating and alive than the world of ordinary things around us. The cool logic of the Renaissance was being replaced by a new mood of deep religious fervor.

The Marriage of Mary, by El Greco.

Light and Dark

Back in Rome, artists were building on the lessons of the Renaissance to take painting to a new level of drama and realism. A vital element in this was the use of light, and the key painter was Michelangelo Merisi da Caravaggio, known simply as Caravaggio (1571–1610). Trained in Milan, Caravaggio went to Rome as a young man in 1592, some 30 years after the death of Michelangelo Buonarroti. He developed a style of painting so distinctive that the many artists who followed his methods were known as "caravaggists."

Real-Life Drama

Caravaggio's work was technically highly polished, and highly realistic. There is little of the Mannerists' exaggeration in his painting. Instead, the drama of his simple scenes comes from the use of a very dark background, contrasting with the strongly lit subject. He shows this even in his early work, such as *Young Bacchus*, a picture of the Roman god of wine, believed actually to be a self-portrait.

Much of Caravaggio's work was commissioned by the various churches in Rome. Typically, he chose dramatic scenes from early Christian history as his subject, such as *The Martyrdom of St. Matthew* or *The Crucifixion of St. Peter*. They portray the horror of the events in a shockingly realistic manner, and the characters depicted are shown as real, ordinary people—not beautified or idealized.

Chiaroscuro

The technical term for the use of strongly contrasting light and dark in painting is "chiaroscuro," from the Italian, meaning light-dark. Oil paints allow artists to use very dark colors, and painters had been exploring the possibilities of deep shadow since the days of Leonardo da Vinci.

Another Italian painter of the Renaissance, Correggio (c.1490–1534), used dramatic lighting and dark shadow, especially to highlight flesh tones. Caravaggio took this technique to its logical conclusion. Unlike most artists before him, he tended to have nothing in the background at all besides darkness, or a darkened wall.

Detail of The Mystic Marriage of St. Catherine with St. Sebastian (c.1520), by Correggio.

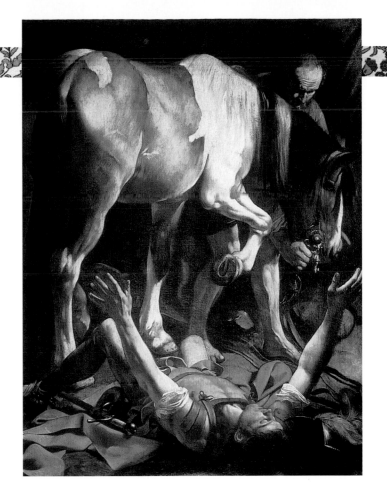

The Conversion of St. Paul is a subject ideally suited to Caravaggio's technique. Paul, a Roman citizen, used to persecute Christians until one day he was struck down by a blinding light on the road to Damascus, and heard Christ's voice calling to him. Caravaggio's interpretation of this scene is utterly believable. The painting looks like real life, which shows real artistic skill, given that the figure of St. Paul is so heavily foreshortened.

Despite all this religious painting, Caravaggio in fact led a wild and scandalous life. In 1606, he killed a man in an argument over a tennis match and had to leave Rome. He traveled to Naples, then Malta and Sicily, and back to Naples again, before dying of malaria at the age of just 39.

Around the World
Japan

After Portuguese navigators reached Japan in 1543, Japan conducted limited trade with Europeans. But fearing the spread of Christianity, the Japanese evicted them in 1639, and a period of more than two centuries of isolation began. European art was not influenced by Japan until trading contacts began again in the late 1800s.

A Japanese screen in black lacquer and gold.

White and Gold

Japanese artists also knew the dramatic effect of light and dark. Lacquer screens provided a backdrop of deep black, on which they painted bold scenes in white and gold. Sometimes they did the reverse, painting in dark colors on a background of white and gold.

The Descent from the Cross (1612–1614), by Rubens.

Rubens and Velázquez

At the close of the 1500s, well after the excitement of the Renaissance had evaporated, Italy was still considered the center of European art. Two of the greatest artists came here to learn. Peter-Paul Rubens (1577–1640), from Antwerp (now in Belgium), spent eight years in Italy, from 1600 to 1608, before returning home. Diego Velázquez (1599–1660), a painter in the court of King Philip IV of Spain, went to Italy twice, in 1629–1631 and 1648–1651.

Baroque

Already a very gifted painter, in Italy, Rubens obtained a new confidence in technique and composition. As a result, his paintings combine technical brilliance with sweeping energy.

Detail of Las Meninas (The Maids of Honor; 1656), by Velázquez.

In his *The Descent from the Cross*, the viewer's eye is led up and down the painting by the diagonal of light. This sense of movement was typical of Rubens, who painted many large canvases in a sketchy, rapid style. But he was also noted for his highly polished paintings for walls and ceilings. It was a style known as Baroque—rich, sumptuous, and loosely based on classical Rome. The Baroque style was adopted by the Roman Catholic Church in its continuing Counter-Reformation, as direct contrast to the severe, frugal simplicity of Protestantism.

Rubens traveled to France, Spain, and England. While in Spain in 1628–1629, he met Velázquez, and they became friends. The mood of Velázquez's work is rather different, but shows a similar technical polish and use of chiaroscuro to dramatic effect. One of his best-loved paintings is *Las Meninas*. The artist, on the left, is painting a portrait of the king and queen, seen in the mirror. What we see is what the king and queen saw, including their daughter, the court dwarf, and a dog.

Mughal Empire

The Mughal emperors came to power in India in 1526. By the reign of Akbar (emperor, 1555-1605), they had created one of the world's most splendid kingdoms. The emperors set up courts that had much in common with the courts of the great Renaissance princes of Europe. They encouraged science and, although Muslim, they held open debates about philosophy and religion. They commissioned magnificent mosques, fortresses, and palaces, including the Taj Mahal, built by Emperor Shah Jahan in 1631-1648 as a tomb for his wife.

Court Painting

The Mughal emperors also encouraged painters. The Mughals painted "miniatures"—detailed pictures on a small scale. Mughal paintings are famous for their delicate touch. They depict carefully observed details from nature, or scenes from court life, often with a charming touch of humor.

Mughal painting therefore gives us a glimpse of the brilliant and rich world of India that Europeans encountered in their trading expeditions. These followed on from the first arrival by Portuguese explorers in 1498. However, the Mughal tradition of painting withered when Shah Aurangzeb, or Alamir, seized the throne in 1658, after imprisoning his father, Shah Jahan. A devout Muslim, Aurangzeb forbade the representation of people or things in art.

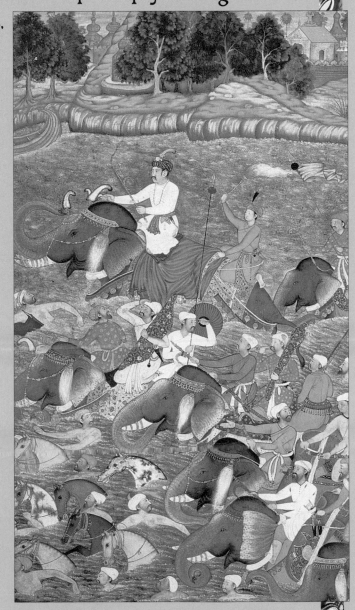

Akbar the Great Crossing the Ganges, a miniature from a Mughal manuscript (c.1600).

Chronology of the Renaissance Period

1303–1305 Giotto paints the frescoes in the Arena Chapel of Padua.

1401 Lorenzo Ghiberti wins the competition to make the doors for the Baptistery of Florence, (completed 1424–1452), considered the first great Renaissance work of Florence.

1434 Beginning of the Medici era in Florence.

1440 The German Johannes Gutenberg uses moveable type to print the Bible, ushering in the modern era of printing.

1484 Botticelli paints his *Birth of Venus*.

1492 Columbus reaches the Americas.

c.1495 Leonardo da Vinci paints *The Last Supper*, in Milan.

1498–1499 Michelangelo sculpts the *Pietà*.

c.1503 Leonardo da Vinci paints the *Mona Lisa*.

1508–1512 Michelangelo paints the ceiling of the Sistine Chapel in the Vatican, in Rome.

1517 Protestant Reformation begins.

1515–1529 War rages for control of Italy as the French capture Milan. Charles V, Holy Roman Emperor and King of Spain, fights with François I of France, captures him in 1525, and sacks Rome in 1527.

1519–1522 First circumnavigation of the globe by an expedition led by the Portuguese navigator Ferdinand Magellan.

1521 Cortés conquers the Aztec empire for Spain.

1526 Foundation of the Mughal empire in India.

1545–1563 At the Council of Trent in Italy, the Roman Catholic Church launches the Counter-Reformation.

1562 Beginning of the Wars of Religion in France.

1600–1608 Rubens lives and works in Italy, before returning to Antwerp.

A Brief History of Art

The earliest known works of art are small carved figurines dating from 30,000 BC. Cave painting dates back to 16,000 BC. Sculpture was the great art form of ancient Greece, from about 500 BC. Greek sculptors attempted to make brilliantly lifelike images.

In Europe, the Renaissance began in the 1300s when artists in Italy rediscovered the culture of the ancient Romans and Greeks. Renaissance artists include painters such as **Giotto** (c.1267–1337), **Masaccio** (1401–1428), **Leonardo da Vinci** (1452–1519), and **Jan van Eyck** (c.1390–1441). **Michelangelo Buonarroti** (1475–1564) made sculpture as fine as anything the ancient Romans or Greeks had produced.

In Europe, Mannerist painters such as **El Greco** (1541–1614) were beginning to put emotion into their paintings. Painters of the Baroque period, such as **Peter-Paul Rubens** (1577–1640), displayed dazzling technical skill and a sense of glamor. The Dutch painter **Rembrandt van Rijn** (1606–1669) showed in his portraits how painting could capture the character of the sitter.

Artists could now paint detailed pictures of reality, but they found that this was not enough. Painters such as **Francisco Goya** (1746–

1828) adapted their style to convey personal expression and emotion. Emotion was a key element of Romanticism. In his late work, **J.M.W. Turner** (1775–1851) used freely applied dashes of color to convey feeling.

In the Realist movement, artists such as **Gustave Courbet** (1819–1877) used their skills to portray real life. In the 1870s, the Impressionists such as **Pierre-Auguste Renoir** (1841–1919), and **Claude Monet** (1840–1926), took Realism in a new direction. They painted outdoors, and rapidly, trying to capture the passing moments of the world. The Post-Impressionists such as **Paul Gauguin** (1848–1903), **Vincent van Gogh** (1853–1890), and **Paul Cézanne** (1839–1906) developed highly individual styles.

In the 1900s, a series of artists' movements followed one after the other. In Cubism, **Pablo Picasso** (1881–1973) explored new ways to look at objects. Expressionism concentrated on putting emotion into painting. The Surrealists, such as **Salvador Dalí** (1904–1989) and **René Magritte** (1898–1967), depicted highly imaginative, dreamlike worlds. The development of abstract art was taken a step further in the works of **Piet Mondrian** (1872–1944), while **Jackson Pollock** (1912–1956) launched Abstract Expressionism. In the late 1900s, Pop artists such as **Andy Warhol** (1926–1987) explored the meaning of art, as did the Minimalists such as **Carl André** (1935–), and installation artists such as **Joseph Beuys** (1921–1986), took art in new directions.

Glossary

Chiaroscuro
The technique of painting using extremes of light and deep shade to produce a three-dimensional effect.

Fresco
The technique of wall-painting in which the paint is applied to areas of wet plaster.

Maestà
A painting of the Madonna seated on a throne with the child Jesus, surrounded by saints and angels.

Mannerism
A style of painting expressing energy and emotion through heightened color, and by distorting the shapes of figures.

Perspective
The illusion of distance in a painting, often achieved by making the parallel lines of the architecture line up with a vanishing point.

Pietà
A painting or sculpture depicting the Virgin Mary after the Crucifixion, holding the dead Christ on her lap.

Sfumato
The painting technique developed by Leonardo da Vinci in which objects are made to merge into each other through shading, instead of having hard lines around them.

Tempera
A kind of paint, usually used on wood panels in which the color is mixed with some kind of gum or glue, usually egg yolk, to make it dry hard.

Vanishing point
In perspective painting, the imaginary point at which all the edges of parallel objects line up.

Index